# FiGHT

## Dee Phillips

Evans

First published in 2009
by Evans Brothers Limited
2A Portman Mansions
Chiltern Street
London W1U 6NR
UK

Printed in Dubai

British Library Cataloguing in Publication Data
Phillips, Dee.
    Fight. -- (Right now)
    1. Graphic novels. 2. Young adult fiction.
    I. Title II. Series
    741.5-dc22
    ISBN-13: 9780237539559

**Developed & Created by** Ruby Tuesday Books Ltd

**Project Director** – Ruth Owen
**Head of Design** – Elaine Wilkinson
**Designer** – Alix Wood
**Editor** – Frances Ridley
**Consultant** – Lorraine Petersen, Chief Executive of NASEN

© Ruby Tuesday Books Limited 2009

### ACKNOWLEDGEMENTS

With thanks to Lorraine Petersen, Chief Executive of NASEN for her help in the development and creation of these books.

Images courtesy of Shutterstock

While every effort has been made to secure permission to use copyright material, the publishers apologise for any errors or omissions in the above list and would be grateful for notification of any corrections to be included in subsequent editions.

It's Saturday night.
I'm outside the club.
If he wants a fight, I'm ready.

# FiGHT

ONE MOMENT CAN CHANGE YOUR LIFE FOREVER

# Ben's Story

I'm getting changed after basketball.
I look in my bag.

I shout, "My phone's gone!"

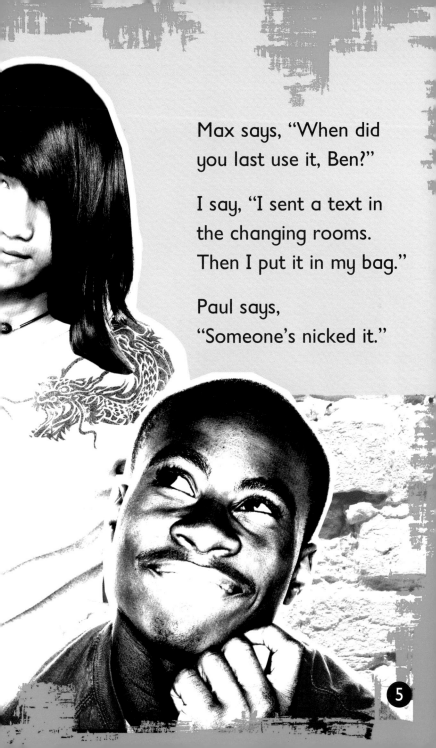

Max says, "When did you last use it, Ben?"

I say, "I sent a text in the changing rooms. Then I put it in my bag."

Paul says, "Someone's nicked it."

5

Later, we go to the youth club.
I'm so angry about my phone.

I feel sick and angry inside.

Paul says, "I saw Kris Black in the changing rooms. He was there with his mates."

Kris and his mates are huddled around the sofas. They are all looking at something and laughing.

# KRIS'S STORY

I'm at the youth club with my mates.

My mate Tyrone says, "Look at
my new iPod, Kris."

He chucks it over and I nearly
drop it. Everybody laughs.

9

Then I see Ben Wilson and his mates.
They're watching me.
What's their problem?

# Ben's Story

The next morning I'm still angry.
At break, I see Paul and Max.

Max says, "I found out Kris Black's dad is in prison. He's a thief."

Paul says, "Maybe it runs in the family."

We walk past Kris Black and Tyrone.
They are laughing, but they
stop when they see me.

I give Kris an angry look.
Is he laughing at me?

# KRIS'S STORY

At break, Tyrone shows me a video
on his iPod. We start laughing.

Then Ben Wilson walks by
with his mates.

17

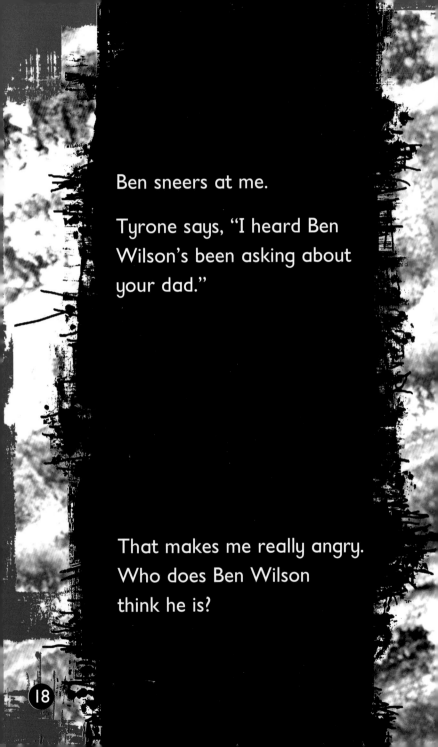

Ben sneers at me.

Tyrone says, "I heard Ben Wilson's been asking about your dad."

That makes me really angry. Who does Ben Wilson think he is?

# Ben's Story

It's Friday night at the youth club.

Paul says, "Don't let Kris Black get away with it. He nicked your phone, Ben."

I feel stupid.
Kris Black is laughing at me.
I say, "I'll smash his laughing face in!"

21

Max says, "You need to sort Kris Black out. He's a dirty thief!"

23

# KRIS'S STORY

It's Friday night at the youth club.
I'm playing pool with Tyrone.

Ben Wilson and his mates are watching us.
They make me so angry.
Nobody says bad stuff about my dad.

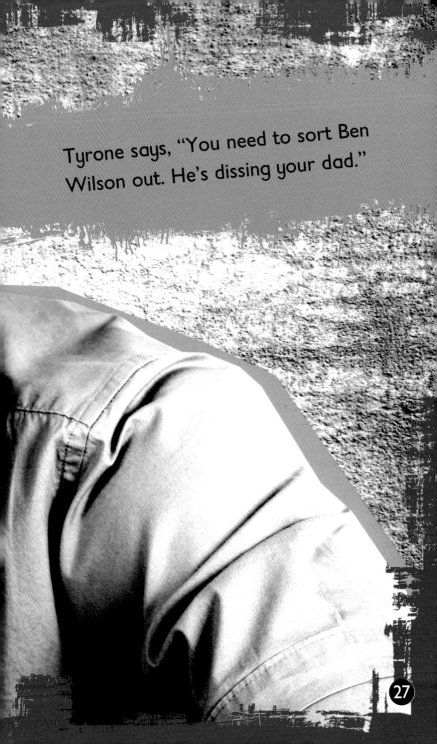

Tyrone says, "You need to sort Ben Wilson out. He's dissing your dad."

# Ben's Story

It's Saturday morning.
We're in town.

Paul says, "I hear Kris Black is looking for a fight."

Max says, "I bet that thief will nick a weapon."

# KRIS'S STORY

It's Saturday afternoon.
I'm at Tyrone's house.

Tyrone says, "I saw Ben Wilson's mates this morning. They say Ben will fight you. He doesn't care if you've got a weapon."

# Ben's Story

It's Saturday afternoon.
We're at Max's house.

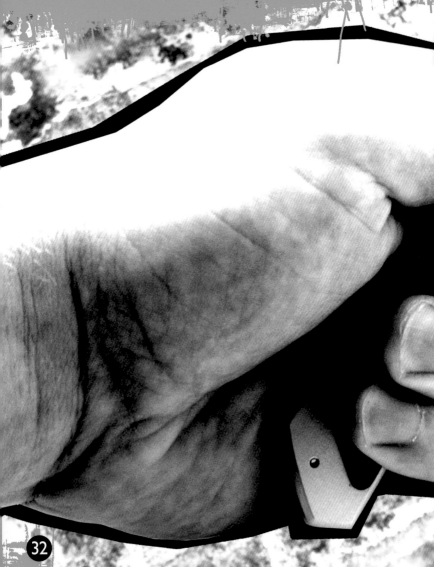

Max says, "I took this from my
dad's fishing box."
He hands me a knife.
"Just in case," he says.

# KRIS'S STORY

It's Saturday night.
I'm outside the club with Tyrone.
I've got a knife in the pocket of my jeans.
Tyrone's cousin gave it to me.
Just in case.

I walk towards the club.
If Kris Black wants a fight, I'm ready.

I'm waiting outside the club.
If Ben Wilson wants a fight, I'm ready.

37

A shove

Swearing

Kicking

# Punching

## SCREAMING

Someone shouts,
"He's got a knife!"

I'm just standing here.
There's blood on my hands.
Someone is shouting, "Call an ambulance!"

I'm lying on the ground.
There's a stabbing pain in my stomach.
Someone is shouting, "Call an ambulance!"

43

# FIGHT – WHAT'S NEXT?

## POSTER POWER
### ON YOUR OWN

Make a poster to stop young people carrying knives.

- Make the headline short and sharp.
- Find or create an eye-catching picture.
- Invent a catchy slogan.
- Include facts and tips.
- Tell people how to get help and advice. You can find help online, for example: *http://www.knifecrimes.org/*.

## FACE TO FACE
### WITH A PARTNER

Decide whether Ben or Kris was wounded in the knife fight. Imagine that the character is rushed to hospital and survives. What would happen if the two characters met up in the future?

- Discuss how they would feel.
- Discuss what they would talk about.
- Role-play the conversation that the two characters have.

# WHiSPERS
## IN A GROUP

A mobile phone goes missing.
Rumour and gossip take over. Soon
two people are having a knife fight.

Create a role-play showing how
rumour and gossip create tension.
For example: *Carl tells Eddie that he
has seen Eddie's girlfriend with her
arm around Will.*

# CRUMPLE BUTTONS
## ON YOUR OWN / WITH A PARTNER / IN A GROUP

Ben feels angry and
upset when he thinks
people are laughing
at him. That's his
"crumple button". Kris feels angry when he thinks people
are dissing his dad. That's his crumple button.

- Keep a diary. Record times
  when you get angry or upset.

- Go through your diary.
  What are your crumple buttons?

- You can control your feelings!
  Think of ways to calm down
  when your crumple button
  is pushed.

Take a deep breath.

Count to 10!

# IF YOU ENJOYED THIS BOOK, TRY THESE OTHER RiGHT NOW! BOOKS.

It's just an old, empty house. Lauren must spend the night inside. Just Lauren and the ghost...

Tonight, Vicky must make a choice. Stay in London with her boyfriend Chris. Or start a new life in Australia.

Dan sees the red car. The keys are inside. Dan says to Andy, Sam and Jess, "Want to go for a drive?"

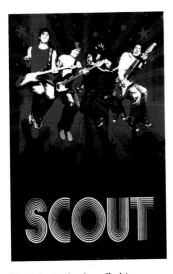

Tonight is the band's big chance. Tonight, a record company scout is at their gig!

Sophie hates this new town. She misses her friends. There's nowhere to skate!

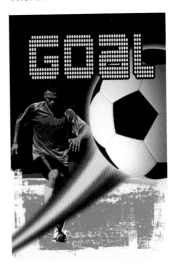

Ed's platoon is under attack. Another soldier is in danger. Ed must risk his own life to save him.

Today is Carl's trial with City. There's just one place up for grabs. But today, everything is going wrong!